The illustrated picture book is one of the most important genres of children's literature. Many brilliant artists have devoted their working lives to creating art that accompanies a text written for children. And while book illustration has been practised for thousands of years, picture book illustration is a fairly new phenomenon.

IBBY (the International Board on Books for Young People), at the heart of whose mandate lies the promotion of books of the highest quality, has been honouring illustrators through the Hans Christian Andersen Awards for nearly forty years. IBBY has also been helping to promote the creation of illustrated children's books in countries where such artistic activity is just beginning to take hold.

In honour of IBBY, and to support its future work, many of the world's greatest illustrators for children – both famous and relatively unknown – have donated a work of art based on a text of their choice drawn from their childhood and culture. The result is a book that celebrates art created for children from around the world. It also celebrates the great variety of traditional writing for children – from riddles, to rhymes, to games, to songs and poetry. Here you will find words in their original language and in English beautifully translated by eminent author, poet and editor, Stan Dragland.

Katherine Paterson, author of Bridge to Terabithia and winner of the 1998 Hans Christian Andersen Award, has contributed a poignant forward.

Under the Spell of the Moon

ART FOR CHILDREN
FROM THE WORLD'S GREAT ILLUSTRATORS

FRANCES LINCOLN
CHILDREN'S BOOKS

Collection copyright © Groundwood Books Ltd. 2004
Illustrations copyright © Jainal Amambing, Mohammed Amous,
Mitsumasa Anno, Rotraut Susanne Berner, Pulak Biswas, Quentin Blake,
Anthony Browne, Carll Cneut, Baba Wagué Diakité, Boris Diodorov,
Philippe Dumas, Ora Eitan, Eva Eriksson, Luis Garay, Marie-Louise Gay,
Piet Grobler, Trina Schart Hyman, Isol, Dušan Kállay, Nasrin Khosravi,
Angela Lago, Alison Lester, Manuel Monroy, Kvĕta Pacovská, Peter Sís,
Marit Törnqvist, Noemí Villamuza, Rosemary Wells, Józef Wilkon,
Vera B. Williams, Linda Wolfsgruber, Ange Zhang, Lisbeth Zwerger, 2004

First published in Canada by Groundwood Books Ltd.

First published in Great Britain in 2006 by
Frances Lincoln Children's Books,
4 Torriano Mews, Torriano Avenue,
London NW5 2RZ
www.franceslincoln.com

British Library Cataloguing in Publication Data available on request

ISBN 1-84507-527-7
ISBN-13: 978-1-84507-527-9

Design by Michael Solomon
Printed and bound in China

Special thanks to:
Lennart Hellsing, Philip de Vos, Jalal Akrami and Rim Banna for permission
to print their poems.
Lynne E. Riggs for her translation of *Good Night, Children* by Mitsumasa Anno.
Allen & Unwin, Australia, for their permission to use excerpts from the text
of *Magic Beach* by Alison Lester.

Foreword by Katherine Paterson
Edited by Patricia Aldana
Texts translated by Stan Dragland

TABLE OF CONTENTS

* traditional
† by the artist

FOREWORD

The beautiful book you are now holding in your hands is the gift of children's illustrators from every continent and even the far-flung islands of the world. I cannot help but wish that Jella Lepman, the founder of the International Board on Books for Young People (IBBY), could see this astounding visual evidence of her dream come true.

In the wake of World War II, Ms. Lepman, a Jewish journalist who had fled her native Germany, was asked to return to her defeated homeland to advise the occupation forces on the cultural and educational needs of women and children who lived in the American zone. She persuaded reluctant generals and bureaucrats that what the children of Germany needed was books — the best in children's books from all over the world — to feed their spirits so starved by years of cruel dictatorship and devastating war. Her first triumph was an exhibition of such books in Munich, which received such an enthusiastic response that she moved on to found an international library of children's books and then to sell an even larger dream — an international organisation that would devote itself to bringing books to children all over the world.

And even that was not her greatest dream. Her ultimate hope was that by nourishing children with the best of books from around the world, they would make friends with children who lived in very different cultures, but who also, like them, longed to grow up in a world of peace. In her autobiography, *A Bridge of Children's Books,* this dream is expressed in a poem:

> Stop telling us of war and destruction,
> The children cry out
> Across the boundaries
> That adults establish.

And they press gloriously on
Into the uncharted future,
Creating again what the other
So mercilessly ruined.

Tragically, Jella Lepman's ultimate dream of a peaceful world for children has yet to come true, but despite international suspicion, terrorism and open warfare, this book you have opened is the bright and hope-filled evidence that the dream of IBBY is alive and well. Through these gifted picture-book artists, *Under the Spell of the Moon* salutes not only the children of the world but the thousands of people in more than sixty-five countries who share Jella Lepman's dream and are carrying out the mandate engraved on her tombstone:

Give them books; give them wings.

Katherine Paterson

INTRODUCTION

Illustration has existed for millennia, the illustrated book for almost as long as there have been books. But the art celebrated in *Under the Spell of the Moon* — illustration aimed specifically at children — is relatively new.

The International Board on Books for Young People (IBBY), whose work Katherine Paterson so eloquently describes in her foreword, is a world-wide organisation. So when we decided that it was time to celebrate artists whose lives have been dedicated to working for children, we knew that we needed to look around the world and find the very best, whether famous and established or new and promising.

Among the artists you will find in this book are many Hans Christian Andersen award winners and nominees who represent countries with rich children's book publishing traditions. Some of these great illustrators are published in many countries. Some, even among the Andersen winners, are still, undeservedly, known primarily in their own countries or regions. The artists also range from giants in the field, who have been working for a lifetime making books for children, to young people who are only beginning to make themselves known but whose work is nonetheless of the highest caliber.

In some parts of the world, picture-book publishing is still limited by economic constraints, market size and, in some cases, the dominance of books published in other countries. Nonetheless, talented illustrators are working, even though not all are yet published.

It was a daunting task to come up with a group of artists of the highest quality whose work represents all the different circumstances of illustration from around the world. Many people helped in this selection. While we did not consult specifically with each IBBY section, it is gratifying to see how many artists who have found their way into this book are represented in the 2004 IBBY

Andersen nominations. The Biennial of Illustrations Bratislava (BIB) and the Noma Concours for Picture Book Illustrations of the Asia/Pacific Cultural Centre for UNESCO (ACCU) were essential in helping to locate less well-known but highly talented illustrators. Both organisations do a wonderful job of finding and supporting talent from outside the main publishing nations.

Finally, the artists in this book are to some extent self-selected by so generously donating their work. Their donation permits a substantial royalty from all sales of this book to be paid to IBBY so that it can continue and expand its work, especially in ensuring that children all over the world can have access to their own wonderful illustrated books.

Each artist was asked to illustrate a text of his or her own choosing, be it a poem, nursery rhyme, song, piece of prose, riddle or street game. The range in the type of text is enormous and often reflects words that were important in the artist's childhood. Because the texts were written in each artist's own language, sometimes by the artists themselves, we asked noted Canadian poet and editor Stan Dragland to render them into wonderful English while retaining their original flavor.

Children who have access to books created especially for them by such outstanding visual artists are extremely lucky. IBBY is working to make this possible for all children and to help create conditions so that artists can emerge in every part of the world and have their books known by children everywhere.

With special thanks to Peter Schneck, Peter Cačko, Elena Iribarren, Tayo Shima, Chieko Suemori, Misako Onuki, Leena Maissen, Liz Page, Noushine Ansari, Amy Kellman, Margaret McElderry, Susanne Padberg, Ken Setterington, Jehan Helou, Sarah Quinn and Michael Solomon for their help in selecting and contacting the artists, and most of all to the illustrators themselves.

Patricia Aldana

12

NOT TO SEE A FOREST FOR A TREE

PRO STROM NEVIDĚT LES

Jerry Hall
Is so small
A rat could eat him
Hat and all.

おやすみなさい、こどもたち

海のむこうに　日が沈む
みんなで帰ろ　草の道
聞いてみようか　あの星に
夕日はどこへ帰るのか

夕日はどこへも　帰らない
さかさの国では　朝日なの
眠りの精が　帰るだけ
山のむこうに　日が昇る

戦の庭に　日が沈み
怪我した子らが　眠るとき
平和の国に　日が昇り
夢みる子らが　目をさます

家中みんなで　ゆうごはん
好き嫌いする子がいても
さかさの国の　あさごはん
パンをわけあう　子もいるの

朝日がのぼる　日が沈む
顔も言葉もちがうけど
遠くの子にも　空があり
同じ地球で　生きてるの

夕日が沈んで　星が出る
地球のどこにも　夜がきて
眠りの精がやってくる
おやすみなさい　こどもたち

Good Night, Children

The sun is setting beyond the sea
Down grassy trails we head toward home.
Oh, evening star, high in the sky
Where is home for the setting sun?

The setting sun goes nowhere home
It is the dawn of another world.
There, the sandman heads for home —
As the sun is rising beyond the hills.

Shadows fall on embattled grounds
Sleep comes to children hurt by war.
In lands of peace, sun climbs the sky.
Children dream, then open their eyes.

Round the supper fare, whole families gather,
And children fuss — don't like this nor that
At breakfast, round the other side of the world
Children share their bread or gruel.

The morning sun rises, the evening sun sets
The faces are different, as are the tongues
But one is the sky that stretches above
For those far and near, all children of Earth.

The setting sun sinks
    The stars twinkle out
        Night comes, and to every corner on Earth
        The sandman is coming.

        Good night, children.

"ŽÁBA SKÁČE
ZO BLÁTA
KÚPIME JI
NA GÁTE

NA JAKÉ?
NA JAKÉ?

NA ZELENÉ
STRAKA-
TÉ!"

THE FROG leaps
Out of the mud.
Let's buy him trousers.
What kind? Which kecks?
Green and tartan.

Květa Pacovská, Czech Republic 19

God natt du sol

God natt du sol! När du går ner
finns inte några färger mer.

Nu lämnar solen land och stad
och alla träd får svarta blad.

Var hund blir svart och svart var katt.
Var tupp blir svart när det blir natt.

Var ko blir svart var so blir svart.
Svart blir min hatt när det blir natt.

God natt du sol! Kom snart igen
Och måla blått på himmelen.

Gör räven röd och gåsen vit.
God natt, kom snart tillbaka hit.

Lennart Hellsing

Marit Törnqvist, The Netherlands, Sweden

Good Night Ye Sun

Good night white hen!
Good night red fox!
The sun he locks
His colour box.

Good night ye sun
Until ye're back
All cats and rats
And bats are black.

All dogs are black
All hogs are black
And frogs are black
Until ye're back.

All fleas are black
All beezzz are black
And geese quack-quack
Are black black-black.

And you are black
And me am black
The world is black
When sun does lack.

The sea does rock
The world to sleep.
Good night ye sun
And hills and sheep!

PROMENONS-NOUS dans les bois
pendant que le loup n'y est pas.
Si le loup y était,
il nous mangerait.
Mais comme il n'y est pas,
il ne nous mangera pas!

INTO THE FOREST let us stray,
While the wolf is far away.
If he were not
He would eat us hot,
But he is away
And won't eat us today.

PRÄSTENS LILLA KRÅKA
SKULLE UT OCH ÅKA
INGEN HADE HON
SOM KÖRDE

WITHOUT ANY guide,
the priest's little crow
went for a ride:

ÄN SLANK HON HIT...

This way first,

ÄN SLANK HON DIT...

That way next,

ÄN SLANK HON -

- NER I DIKET!

Finally — whoo!
Into the ditch.

Five in a Bed

There were five in a bed
And the little one said
"Roll over, roll over"
So they all rolled over
And one fell out

There were four in a bed
And the little one said
"Roll over, roll over"
So they all rolled over
And one fell out

Vera B. Williams, USA

There were three in a bed
And the little one said
"Roll over, roll over"
So they all rolled over
And one fell out

There were two in a bed
And the little one said
"Roll over, roll over"
So they all rolled over
And one fell out

There was one in a bed
And the little one said
"I'm lonely"

A LITTLE pointed cap
Dancing in the ring!
Three threes are nine.
You know what I mean.
Three threes are nine
And one more is ten.
Stop, cap, stop!
It shook and shook itself,
Tossed the sack
Behind its back.
Clap, clap hands —
The two of us are friends.

EINE KLEINE Zipfelmütze
geht in unserm Kreis herum.
Dreimal drei ist neune,
ihr wisst ja wie ich's meine.
Dreimal drei ist neun,
und eins dazu ist zehn.
Zipfelmütze, bleib stehn, bleib stehn!
Sie schüttelt sich, sie rüttelt sich,
sie wirft ihr Säcklein hinter sich,
sie klatschen in die Hand,
wir beide sind verwandt.

NASRIN
KHOSRAVI · 2003

30   *Nasrin Khosravi, Iran*

THE OLD WOMAN in our tale
Wears her hair in forty braids.
Each spring on her verandah she waits
For Amoo Norooz,
And each time falls asleep
Under the spell of the moon.
Then Amoo Norooz arrives,
Touches with love
Her offering of fruit,
Chooses a red apple, takes a bite,
Then places a narcissus in her hair.
There is one God only,
One God and a grandmother
With her grey hair worn
In forty braids.

چل گیس قصه‌ی ما خواب میمونه
توی ایوون می خوابه ، اسیر مهتاب میمونه
عمونوروز میاد و یواشکی ،
به هفت سین اش دس می که
با خودش یه شاخه نرگس میاره
میون موهای چل گیس می ذاره
بعد شم دس می بره تو هفت سین و ،
یه سیب سرخ گاز می زنه

From "Amoo Norooz"
retold by Jalal Akrami

31

My FEET on your head.

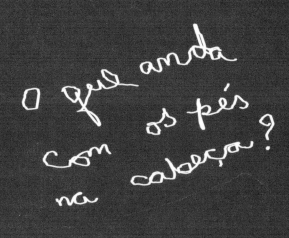

O que anda
com os pés
na cabeça?

[a lousa]

Angela Lago

THE MORE of me you remove, the bigger I get.

o que quanto mais se tira mais cresce?

buraco

34   *Trina Schart Hyman, USA*

THROUGH ALL the pleasant meadow-side
The grass grew shoulder-high
Till the shining scythes went far and wide
And cut it down to dry.

These green and sweetly smelling crops
They led in waggons home;
And they piled them here in mountain tops
For mountaineers to roam.

Here is Mount Clear, Mount Rusty-Nail,
Mount Eagle and Mount High;—
The mice that in these mountains dwell,
No happier are than I!

Oh, what a joy to clamber there,
Oh, what a place for play,
With the sweet, the dim, the dusty air,
The happy hills of hay!

Robert Louis Stevenson
"The Hayloft" from *A Child's Garden of Verses*

A LA MAR fui por naranjas,
cosa que la mar no tiene;
me dejaron mojadita
las olas que van y vienen.

Ay, mi dulce amor,
ese mar que ves, tan bello,
ay mi dulce amor,
ese mar que ves tan bello, es un traidor.

Isol, Argentina

I WENT TO THE OCEAN for oranges,
One thing the ocean lacks;
From the waves that roll and roll
I came all sodden back.

O my darling,
The ocean so lovely to see,
O my darling,
The ocean's a traitor to me.

He thought he saw an Elephant
That practised on a fife:
He looked again, and found it was
A letter from his wife.
"At length I realise" he said,
"The bitterness of Life!"

He thought he saw a Buffalo
Upon the chimney-piece:
He looked again, and found it was
His Sister's Husband's Niece.
"Unless you leave this house", he said,
"I'll send for the Police!"

He thought he saw a Rattlesnake
That questioned him in Greek:
He looked again, and found it was
The Middle of Next Week.
"The one thing I regret" he said,
"Is that it cannot speak!"

ἀνηβῶ στόν οὐρανόν
νὰ φωνάξω τρεῖς φωνές

He thought he saw a Banker's Clerk
Descending from the bus:
He looked again, and found it was
A Hippopotamus:
"If this should stay to dine", he said
"There won't be much for us!"

38   *Philippe Dumas, France*

He thought he saw a Kangaroo
That worked a coffee-mill:
He looked again, and found it was
  A Vegetable-Pill.
"Were I to swallow this," he said,
"I should be very ill!"

He thought he saw a Coach-and-Four
That stood beside his bed
He looked again, and found it was
  A Bear without a Head.
"Poor thing," he said, "poor silly thing!
It's waiting to be fed!"

He thought he saw an Albatross
That fluttered round the lamp:
He looked again, and found it was
  A Penny-Postage-Stamp.
"You'd best be getting home," he said:
"The nights are very damp!"

He thought he saw a Garden-Door
That opened with a Key:
He looked again, and found it was
A Double Rule of Three
"And all its mystery," he said,
"Is clear as day to me!"

Philippe Dumas

'K ZAG twee beren
Broodjes smeren
Oh het was een wonder
't Was een wonder, boven wonder
Dat die beren smeren konden
Hie hie hie, Ha ha ha
'k Stond er bij en ik keek ernaar

I SAW two bears
Buttering buns.
O what a wonder —
Wonder over wonder —
Buttering bears.
Hi hi hi, ho ho ho
And I right there,
Taking it in.

At My Birthday Party

At my birthday party
I had chocolate cake,
And cheesecake,
And fruitcake,
And ginger cake,
And fudge cake.
After that I had stummercake.

42 *Anthony Browne, UK*

44   *Pulak Biswas, India*

Rhinoceros

HORN LIKE A DAGGER,
Skin so rough —
The rhinoceros's body
Is very, very tough.

Ťap, ťap, ťapušky,

CLAP, CLAP *your hands,*
The cats were picking pears,
They tore their coats of fur,
They hung them on the gate, and
The tailor fixed them quick.

išli mačky na hrušky, *podriapali kožúšky,*
povešali na vráta,
príde drotár, popláta.

Vice Versa

EIN HASE sitzt auf einer Wiese,
des Glaubens, niemand sähe diese.

Doch, im Besitze eines Zeisses,
betrachtet voll gehaltnen Fleisses

vom vis-à-vis gelegnen Berg
ein Mensch den kleinen Löffelzwerg.

Ihn aber blickt hinwiederum
ein Gott von fern an, mild und stumm.

Christian Morgenstern

THE HARE in the meadow is secure:
Nobody sees him, he is sure.

But very closely from afar,
On the mountain over there,

A man with his binoculars
Is watching little floppy ears,

And he in turn is being spied
By a gentle, silent god.

EIN HASE SITZT AUF EINER WIESE
DES GLAUBENS NIEMAND SÄHE DIESE
DOCH IM BESITZE EINES ZEISSES
BETRACHTET VOLL FLEISSES
VON VIS-A-VIS GELE
EIN MENSCH DEN KLEINEN LÖFFELZWERG
IHN ABER BLICKT HINWIEDERUM
EIN GOTT VON FERN AN MILD UND STUMM

ח.נ. בְּיַאלִיק

פָּרָשׁ

רוּץ, בֶּן-סוּסִי,
רוּץ וּדְהָר!
רוּץ בַּבִּקְעָה,
טוּס בָּהָר!

רוּצָה, טוּסָה,
יוֹם וָלָיְל, —
פָּרָשׁ אֲנִי
וּבֶן-חָיִל!

Rider

RUN, my colt,
Canter, gallop,
Over meadow,
Over hilltop.

Run, fly
On light wings, high.
And I your rider —
My oh my!

H. N. Bialik

Suzan na

Suzan na,
So yi pan,
Suzan na,
K'a ye kamalen ye.

Suzan na,
So n'a musso yi pan,
Suzan na,
K'u ye kamalenw ye.

Over the Fence

Over the fence, the high
    grey fence —
The tall white horse
Leaps the high grey fence
To boast of his mighty
    youth.

Over the fence, the tall grey fence —
A yearling colt and a yearling mare
Gracefully leap the high grey fence
In the prime of their mighty youth.

Secret City

At the Firehouse
On 83rd street,
There's a secret City near people's feet
Saints in bottled candles, talking,
Right down there where the people are walking.

People whisper, "Thank you!" Meaning,
"You, against the firetruck, leaning,
Best of our best, Bravest of Brave!
God bless you for all the lives you save!"

Saints in bottles of colored glass
Stay with the ones who walk on past.
Winky, blinky on the dark street,
Secret City at people's feet.

At our beach,
at our magic beach,
we swim in the sparkling sea,
surfing and splashing
and jumping the waves,
shrieking and laughing with glee.

At our beach,
at our magic beach,
we search in the clear, warm pools,
peering at starfish,
limpets and crabs,
and tiny fish darting in schools.

At our beach,
at our magic beach,
we play in the sand for hours,
digging and building,
with buckets and spades,
invincible castles and towers.

At our beach,
at our magic beach,
we rock in the tangerine boat,
paddling out to the end of the line,
then drifting back to the float.

At our beach,
at our magic beach,
we bask in the glow of the fire.
The moon makes a silvery path on the sea,
and the waves come to the shore with a sigh.

At our beach,
at our magic beach,
the old bed is cosy and wide.
To the sounds of the ocean
we sleep through the night...
...adrift on the evening tide.

Alison Lester, Australia 57

Bumi karya
Tuhan yang indah

DI LANGIT sana bertingkat
pelangi
Bayu putih dan kelabu bercumbuan mesra
Mereka tidak malu mendakap gunung-gunung
Mereka mencium rimba,
Mereka bersatu dan saling mengasihi
Ilusi irama alam.

Di rimba sana
Rerama berterbangan bebas
Mereka membelai dan mencium bunga-bunga
Mereka saling merindui.
Mereka saling mengasihi, asmara berpanjangan
Bumi karya Tuhan yang indah.

Di lembah sana mereka bercanda
Di antara lautan bendang keemasan
Burung-burung berkicauan riang ria
Tanda pesta menjelang tiba
Mereka berbudaya
Mereka berharmoni
Mereka berdamai
Mereka saling mengasihi
Di bumi karya Tuhan
yang indah.
Ucap syukurlah
sepanjang zaman.

The Beautiful
Land of God

HIGH IN THE SKY, rainbows kiss
The white and grey clouds.
They embrace the mountains freely,
And kiss the jungles.
Rainbows join everything in nature
To everything else. Rainbows
Rhyme everything.

Down in the distant jungle
Butterflies flutter by one another,
Passionately kissing the flowers —
Butterflies and flowers deeply and always in love
In the Land of God.

Down in the valley they play
Among the waves of golden crops.
They cry out with delight to see the foraging birds.
They know the celebration is about to start.
They cavort in all the colours.
They dance to the rhythm of peace,
Deeply in love,
Forever thankful
For the beautiful Land
of God.

拉大锯，扯大锯，姥姥家，唱大戏，接闺女，请女婿

小外孙子也要去。拉大锯，扯大锯，姥姥家，唱大戏。

60 *Ange Zhang, China*

PLAY THE violin, beat the drum:
Opera night at Grandma's house.

Greetings, daughter.
Welcome, son-in-law.
My grandson, enjoy the evening.

¿CUÁL ES la fruta que tiene la semilla
por fuera?

WHAT FRUIT keeps its seed outside?

DE SANTA tengo el san,
de dia tengo el dia,
soy roja y blanca,
y de sangre fría.

GREENISH skin,
Cold blood within:
My flesh is red
And sweet as sin.

la cuna de mi niño
se mece sola
como en el campo verde
las amapolas

My baby's cradle
Rocks itself —
Poppies nod
In a field of green.

ELKE outjie,
het sy lied:
krokodil
en zoeiii-muskiet,
elke
kokkerot
of sysie
met sy
eie sysiewysie.
Elke gogga, elke mensie
elke omie met sy pensie
moet kan skinner, krys of kweel
kwinkeleer of koer of neul.
Of dit fraai, of goor of gek is,
jy moet sing soos jy gebek is.

Philip de Vos

EVERYBODY has a song,
be it short or be it long,
in the right or in the wrong key,
like the hee-haw of a donkey,
twitter, tweet, tu-whit, tu-whoo,
howl or growl or quack or moo.
Everyone has a song
and must sing it all life long.
Don't be silent
nor afraid,
you must sing
as you've been made.

Piet Grobler, South Africa

Wlazł kotek na płotek i mruga…
Piękna to plosenka, niedługa.
Niedługa, niekrótka, lecz w sam raz,
zaśpiewaj, koteczku, jeszcze raz!

On a short fencepost, a little cat clears its throat...
A pleasant song, and not too long by a note,
Not too long, not too short, but precise.
One more serenade please, little cat — it's nice.

عنا حمار .. شكله لطيف .. بس بالليل مكركعنا
مقضيها ينهق تنهيق..يخرب شرهُ مغلبنا
يا حرام .. يا حرام .... الله يصبّر هالحمار

في يوم من الضُبحيات راحلو جدي تا يهديه
لاقاه واقف زعلان .. معنّد تا يمشي
يا حرام .. يا حرام .... الله يعقّل هالحمار

أجا اليوم الثاني كمان... لا نام ولا نيمنا
إنزلنالو مع الجيران .. يا عمي شو مفقعنا
شو بدك يا حمار ... لو تحكي وتخلصنا
بنُص الليل وعز النهار ... ما مخلينا نتهنى

أجا يوم من الأيام .. تعرفلو على حماره
راق بالو وصار ينام.. وهديت من بعدو الحاره

لو عارفين من زمان ..كان ما خليناه حيران
كان عرفناه على حماره ... وطمّن بالو وطمَنا

عنا حمار .. شكله لطيف .. بس بالليل مكركعنا
مقضيها ينهق تنهيق..يخرب شرُه مغلبنا
يا حرام .. يا حرام .... الله يصبّر هالحمار

We have a donkey. He looks really cute,
But every single night he goes on a toot.
He brays and brays the whole night through:
Lord love a duck! What are we to do?

    Poor donkey, wretched brute. Please, God,
    Won't you make him mute.

He brays and brays the whole night long.
Nobody sleeps through that kind of song.
The neighbours know you're driving us nuts;
Tells us what you want, no ifs, ands or buts.

    Poor donkey, wretched beast. Please, God,
    Make him hoarse at least.

Finally, in the early hours,
Grandfather tried to use his powers,
Persuasive powers to settle him down,
The irate donkey with his donkey frown.

    No dice. Now it's bray all day.
    If we don't get some rest, there'll be hell to pay.

At last, at last! What do you know!
He's calmed right down, the so-and-so.
He's catching forty winks, and so are we,
And the answer to the riddle was a donkey She!

    If we had known what irked him so,
    We'd have given him a girlfriend ages ago.

We have a donkey. He looks so great,
And he's a good donkey now, provided with a mate.

Rim Banna

ENNE DENNE
DUBBE DENNE
DUBBE DENNE
DALIA

EBBE BEBBE
BEMBIO
BIO BIO BUFF

Eenie, meenie, minie, moe,
Catch a tiger by the toe,
If he hollers, let him go,
Eenie, meenie, minie, moe.

Ай, дуду, дуду, дуду!
Идёт ворон по лугу,
Он играет во трубу.
Труба точеная
Позолоченая.

I mweEE-ah, I da-dat *dao*!
Mister Raven, bopping in the field,
Trumpet wailing,
Shapely trumpet,
Horn of gold.

ABOUT THE ARTISTS

JAINAL AMAMBING was born in Kudat, Sabah, in Malaysia. He has won numerous prizes for illustration in Malaysia and was an Encouragement Prize winner at the 11th Noma Concours, the second prize winner at the 12th Noma Concours and a runner-up prize winner at the 13th Noma Concours. He currently works as a freelance artist, cartoonist and children's book illustrator in Kudat.

MUHAMMED AMOUS, a Palestinian children's book illustrator, was born in Jerusalem where he currently lives with his wife and two children. He studied math at Bethlehem University until the university was closed as a result of the Palestinian uprising in 1989. He then began his career as a freelance illustrator. His books for children include *Nos Nsais*, a Palestinian fairy tale, and *Dima*, a collection of stories for children. He has also worked as an art director for several advertising agencies, animation producer for Palestinian Sesame Street (*Hikayat Semsem*) and actor for the Nakhleh Esheber children's theatre. He is the co-founder of the Nakhleh Esheber Institute for art production.

MITSUMASA ANNO, one of Japan's leading illustrators and book designers, was born in western Japan and worked as a primary school teacher before beginning his career as an illustrator. He has published more than 140 books that are well-loved around the world. Anno has been awarded the Grand Prix of Graphics in Bologna, a Golden Apple at the Biennial of Illustrations Bratislava (twice), the Kate Greenaway Medal, the Brooklyn Museum of Art Books for Children citation and many Japanese picture-book prizes. He won the Hans Christian Andersen Award in 1984. Mitsumasa Anno now lives in Tokyo.

ROTRAUT SUSANNE BERNER was born in Stuttgart, Germany. She studied graphic design and spent two years working for several publishing houses before becoming an independent illustrator and designer. The books she has written and illustrated for children have won international acclaim, including the Deutscher Jugendliteraturpreis for her illustrations in *Love That Dog* by Sharon Creech, the Silveren Penseel (the Netherlands) and nominations for the Astrid Lindgren Award and the 2004 Hans Christian Andersen Award (for which she was a finalist). She now lives and works in Munich.

PULAK BISWAS is one of the most senior children's book illustrators in India. Based in Delhi, he began his art career more than forty years ago, working for several advertising agencies before becoming a freelance artist in 1981. He now concentrates on painting and children's book illustration, which he considers to be his true vocation. During his long career, Pulak Biswas has worked for a number of publishers in India and overseas. Among other awards, his book *Tiger On a Tree* (Tara Books) won a plaque at the Biennial of Illustrations Bratislava. He is the first Indian to receive this prize.

QUENTIN BLAKE was born in Sidcup, Kent. After studies in education and English literature, his first children's book was published in 1960. Since then he has illustrated more than 250 books by many writers – notably John Yeoman, Russell Hoban, Joan Aiken, Michael Rosen and, most famously, Roald Dahl. He is also well known for his own picture books such as *Clown* and *Zagazoo*. Quentin Blake was a tutor at the Royal College of Art from 1965 to 1988, and for eight of those years was head of the Illustration Department. He was made an OBE in 1988. In 1999 he was appointed the first Children's Laureate, and in 2002 he was made a Chevalier des Arts et des Lettres, and the Quentin Blake Europe School in Berlin was named for him. He was also awarded the Hans Christian Andersen Award. Quentin Blake now lives and works in London, England.

ANTHONY BROWNE studied graphic design at Leeds College of Art and worked as a medical artist and a greeting card designer before writing and illustrating his first picture book, *Through the Magic Mirror*, in 1976. Since then he has published thirty-six books, including the Willy series. He won the Kate Greenaway

Medal for *Gorilla* and *Zoo*, and the Kurt Maschler Award for *Alice's Adventures in Wonderland*, *Voices in the Park* and *Gorilla*. In 2000 he became the first British illustrator to win the Hans Christian Andersen Award. Anthony Browne was the illustrator-in-residence at Tate Britain in 2002, and has had exhibitions of his pictures in Mexico, Germany, Japan, the USA, Colombia, Venezuela, Taiwan, Holland, Belgium and France. He now lives in Kent, England.

CARLL CNEUT was born in a small village in Belgium near the Belgian-French border. He began illustrating children's books in 1996, after studying graphic design at the Saint-Lucas Arts School in Ghent and working as an art director for an advertising agency. Since then he has won both Belgian and international awards, including a plaque at the Biennial of Illustrations Bratislava, and an honourable mention for the BolognaRagazzi Award. In 2002 he made his writing debut with *The Amazing Love Story of Mr. Morf*. He now lives in Ghent, where he illustrates children's books for publishing companies in Europe and North America.

BABA WAGUÉ DIAKITÉ is an artist and storyteller whose images on glazed ceramic tiles have won him high acclaim. His picture book, *The Hunterman and the Crocodile*, is a Coretta Scott King Award Honor Book, and *The Magic Gourd* received an award from Parent's Guide to Children's Media. His vibrant illustrations also appear in *The Hatseller and the Monkeys*, *The Pot of Wisdom* and, most recently, *Jamari's Drum*. He has made it his life's work to share the culture of his homeland with the people of his adopted home. Baba Wagué Diakité is presently building the Toguna Cultural Centre in Bamako, Mali, to bring people from the West in contact with Malian artists and culture. He grew up in Mali and now lives in Portland, Oregon.

BORIS DIODOROV lives in Moscow, where he was named People's Artist of the Russian Federation in 1999, the highest honour for a contribution to Russian culture. He started working with publishing houses in 1958. Since then he has illustrated more than 300 books. His illustrations for Selma Lagerlöf's *The Wonderful Travels of Nils Holgersson* brought him international recognition, including a Golden Apple at the Biennial of Illustrations Bratislava and the Silver Medal at the International

Book Art Exposition in Leipzig. More recently, he has illustrated the Hans Christan Andersen tales *La petite sirène*, winner of a plaque in Bratislava, and *La reine des neiges* for Albin Michel in France. He is a three-time nominee for the Hans Christian Andersen Award, and was a finalist in 2000. In 2001 he received the Grand Prix of the International Hans Christian Andersen Award Committee in Odense, Denmark. He has twice been a member of the international jury of the Biennial of Illustrations Bratislava, and is currently a professor cathedra of illustration and graphic art at the University of Poligrat.

PHILIPPE DUMAS was born in Cannes, France, and now lives in Geneva, Switzerland. After studies at the École des métiers d'art and the École des Beaux-Arts in Paris, he began a career dedicated to writing, illustrating, printing and binding books. Dumas has illustrated the stories of many fine contemporary writers, as well as classics by Victor Hugo, Guy de Maupassant and Gustave Flaubert. He has also written and illustrated more than two dozen books for children and is especially well known for his playful drawings for popular poetry, nursery rhymes and songs. Awards for his work include the Prix Sorcière, the Grand Prix de la Ville de Paris, the Prix graphique Loisirs Jeunes and two nominations for the Hans Christian Andersen Award. He is one of the few artists to be nominated for his work as both an author and an illustrator.

ORA EITAN lives in Jerusalem and has illustrated many Hebrew and English picture books. Her work has earned her great critical acclaim on both sides of the Atlantic, including a nomination for the Hans Christian Andersen Award. Her picture books include *Inch by Inch*, *Cowboy Bunnies* and *Astro Bunnies*. When not in her studio, Ora Eitan teaches at the Bezalel Academy of Art and Design.

EVA ERIKSSON was born in Halmstad, on the southwest coast of Sweden. Before becoming a full-time illustrator, she studied art and art education, and worked in a variety of jobs, including teaching Swedish to immigrants and designing signs in Dublin. Throughout her career, she has alternated between writing and illustrating. In 1978 she published her first book as both author and illustrator – later published in English as *Hocus Pocus*. Eva Eriksson is also a long-time member of the Swedish section of

IBBY. Her honours include three nominations for the Hans Christian Andersen Award, including one in 2004, a plaque from the Biennial of Illustrations Bratislava, and the Astrid Lindgren Award. She now lives in Älta, Sweden.

LUIS GARAY is a well-known Latin American illustrator whose vibrant work appears in *Jade and Iron*, *A Handful of Seeds*, *Popul Vuh* and, most recently, *Cousins* by Elisa Amado. His honours include a Bulletin Blue Ribbon award and the Illustrated Children's and Youth Book Prize. After living in Toronto for many years, he is now returning to his native Nicaragua.

MARIE-LOUISE GAY is a world-renowned author and illustrator of children's books. She has won many prestigious awards including the Governor General's Award, the Amelia Frances Howard-Gibbon Award, the Mr. Christie's Book Award and the Elizabeth Mrazik-Cleaver Picture Book Award. She also received a nomination for the 2004 Hans Christian Andersen Award. Her books have been translated into more than twelve languages and are loved by children all over the world. Her most recent book in the now famous Stella series is *Stella, Princess of the Sky*. Marie-Louise Gay lives with her family in Montreal.

PIET GROBLER lives in Stellenbosch in the Cape winelands of South Africa with his wife and baby daughter. He has earned degrees in theology and journalism and recently completed a Masters degree in Fine Art. A designer and illustrator for fourteen years, he has focused on illustrating picture books since 1999. His picture books have earned him many awards, including two second prizes at the Noma Concours, the Octogone de Chêne (France) and a plaque at the Biennial of Illustrations Bratislava.

TRINA SCHART HYMAN was born in Philadelphia, and decided at an early age to be an artist. She studied illustration and printmaking at art colleges in Philadelphia, Boston, and Stockholm, Sweden. A children's book illustrator for more than 30 years, she gained a reputation as one of North America's most outstanding illustrators. Among other honours, she was awarded the Boston Globe/Horn Book Award for illustration, two Caldecott Honours and the Caldecott Medal for

Illustration for her book *Saint George and the Dragon*. Sadly, Trina died in 2005.

ISOL was born in Buenos Aires, Argentina, where she currently lives and works as an illustrator for children's books, newspapers and magazines. Among her many books for children are *Vida de Perros*, *Cosas que pasan* and *El globo*, which she both wrote and illustrated, published by Fondo de Cultura Economica, Mexico. She has published her work in Spain, France, Mexico and Argentina. In 2003 she won a Golden Apple at the Biennale of Illustrations Bratislava. Her book *El cuento de Navidad de Auggie Wren* (Sudamericana), written by Paul Auster, obtained a Special Mention from The White Ravens 2004.

DUŠAN KÁLLAY was born in Bratislava, Slovakia. Since completing studies in art, he has devoted himself to graphic art, book illustration, painting, stamp design and cartooning. Among his many honours are the Hans Christian Andersen Award and the Grand Prize at the 1983 Biennial of Illustrations Bratislava, awarded for his illustrations for Lewis Carroll's *Alice in Wonderland*. He has illustrated many books for both children and adults and is considered the foremost Slovak illustrator. He continues to live and work in Bratislava.

NASRIN KHOSRAVI was born in Tehran, Iran. She has illustrated more than thirty books for children since her first book was published in 1976. Winner of the Grand Prize at the Noma Concours in Japan, she has also been nominated for the Hans Christian Andersen Award and has received honours in Italy, Germany, Iran, Austria, India, France, Spain and Slovakia. Nasrin Khosravi now lives with her family in Toronto.

ANGELA LAGO was born in Belo Horizonte, Brazil. She has been writing and illustrating books for children for almost twenty years. Most recently, she has been working with interactive animation and new media. Awards for her work include a plaque from the Biennial of Illustrations Bratislava, the Segundo Prémio Iberamericano de Illustración and the Octogone de Ardoise from the Centre International d'Etudes en Littératures de Jeunesse in Paris. She also received a nomination for the 2004 Hans Christian Andersen Award, her second nomination for this award. She continues to live and work in Belo Horizonte.

ALISON LESTER lives and works in Nar Nar Goon North in West Gippsland, Australia. Her picture books mix imaginary worlds with everyday life, encouraging children to believe in themselves and celebrate the differences that make them special. *The Quicksand Pony* and *Magic Beach*, published by Allen & Unwin, are favourites in many Australian households. Her books have received nominations for the Australian Booksellers' Association Book of the Year Award and Australia's National Book Award, among others. As an art teacher, Alison Lester spends part of every year travelling to schools in remote areas, using her books to help children write and illustrate their own stories.

MANUEL MONROY is a talented young Mexican illustrator who studied graphic design, specialising in illustration, at the Universidad Autónoma Metropolitana. He has won several awards, including the Quorum Prize and the Encouragement Prize from the Noma Concours in Japan. He has illustrated two highly acclaimed titles, *Daybreak, Nightfall* and *Rooster Gallo*, both by poet Jorge Luján. Manuel Monroy lives in Mexico City.

KVĚTA PACOVSKÁ was born in Prague in the Czech Republic, where she lives and works today. Winner of the 1992 Hans Christian Andersen Award, she is recognised internationally for her exploratory work in the field of modern illustration, book concept and design. She has illustrated more than fifty books for children, which have been translated into German, French, English, Japanese and many other languages. For the past decade she has devoted her time exclusively to the creation of books as complete works of art — three-dimensional, tactile art objects. Her long list of international honours includes the Grand Prize and a Golden Apple at the Biennial of Illustrations Bratislava, the BolognaRagazzi Award, the Deutscher Jugendliteraturpreis and the Guttenbergpreis in Leipzig.

PETER SÍS is one of the world's most distinguished picture book author-illustrators. Born in Czechoslovakia, he studied painting and filmmaking at the Academy of Applied Arts in Prague and at the Royal College of Art in London. He has written and illustrated many award-winning books for children, including *Starry Messenger: Galileo Galilei* and *Tibet Through the Red Box* (both Caldecott Honor medal winners), as well as *Madlenka*, *Madlenka's Dog* and *The Tree of Life*. He has won numerous other accolades many times over, including the New York Times Best Illustrated Book Award, the Boston Globe/Horn Book Award and Society of Illustrator medals. In 2003 Peter Sís was named a MacArthur Fellow. He lives in New York with his wife and two children.

MARIT TÖRNQVIST was born in Uppsala, Sweden, and moved to the Netherlands when she was five years old. After completing her studies in illustration at the Amsterdam Rietveld Academy, she returned to Sweden where she collaborated with author Astrid Lindgren on four picture books, including *The Red Bird*, which was published in 2003 in several countries. She has also designed scenery based on Astrid Lindgren's work for the Junibacken fairy-tale house in Stockholm. Marit Törnqvist was awarded the Silver Griffel Award for her picture book *Klein verhaal over liefde* and was selected for the IBBY Honour List in 2000 for her illustrations for *Helden op sokken* by Annie Makkink. She now lives and works in Amsterdam.

NOEMÍ VILLAMUZA studied at the University of Salamanca and graduated in arts in 1994. Since 1997 she has been working as an illustrator and teaching at the Bau School of Design. She has illustrated twenty books for children, most recently, *De verdad que no podía* and *Me gusta*, published by Editorial Kokinos in Madrid. She was a finalist for the Premio Nacional de Ilustración in 2002. Noemí Villamuza lives in Barcelona.

ROSEMARY WELLS was born in New York City. After studying at the Museum School in Boston, she began a career as a book designer before becoming a full-time illustrator. Since she published her first picture book in 1968, Rosemary Wells' work has been recognised for its strong sense of humour and realism and its gently rebellious approach to childhood. Her books have received numerous honours, including a New York Times Book Review Best Illustrated Book of the Year and a Publisher's Weekly Best Book of the Year Award for *My Very First Mother Goose*. She lives and works outside New York City.

JÓZEF WILKOŃ was born near Krakow in Poland. Since

JÓZEF WILKOŃ was born near Krakow in Poland. Since completing studies in art, he has worked as an illustrator and graphic designer. Over the years he has designed and illustrated more than one hundred books for children and adults in his native Poland, and sixty-five other books published in countries such as France, Japan, Germany and Switzerland. Still active as a painter, sculptor, and set and tapestry designer, he has received nominations for the 2000 and 2004 Hans Christian Andersen Awards. Other awards include the gold medal at the International Book Fair in Leipzig, the Grand Prize at the Biennial of Illustrations Bratislava, the Primero Grafico in Bologna, and the Owl Prize in Japan. He now lives and works near Warsaw.

VERA B. WILLIAMS was born in Hollywood, California, and moved to the Bronx, New York, as a young child. Since her days as a student at Music and Art High School in NYC and then at the Bauhaus-inspired Black Mountain College in North Carolina, she has been active as a writer, graphic artist, educator, parent and grandparent and in work for peace and justice. She was one of the founders of both the Gate Hill Cooperative Community and the experimental Collaberg School. Among other honours, she has received two Caldecott Honour Medals and Globe and Horn Book awards for both fiction and poetry. Her books have been published in many countries, including China, Denmark, France, Japan, Korea, Sweden and the United Kingdom. Nominated for the 2004 Hans Christian Andersen Award, Vera B. Williams lives in New York City.

LINDA WOLFSGRUBER studied art in Italy. Her highly original works have been exhibited throughout Europe as well as in Japan, New York and San Diego. Her books have been translated into fifteen languages and she has won many prizes, including Austria's 1995 prize for children's book illustration. She has recently illustrated *Inanna: From the Myths of Ancient Sumer*, written by Kim Echlin, and *Stories from the Life of Jesus*, written by Celia Barker Lottridge. Linda Wolfsgruber lives in Vienna.

ANGE ZHANG is an artist and an internationally known theatre designer who worked with the National Opera Theatre in Beijing before moving to Canada. He has illustrated many children's books including *Thor* (*Winter Rescue* in the U.S.), which won the Mr. Christie's Book Award, and *The Fishing Summer*, *The Stone Boat* and *The Kid Line*, written by Teddy Jam. Most recently he has written and illustrated *Red Land, Yellow River*, his own story of growing up in China during the Cultural Revolution. Ange now works in animation and lives with his family in Toronto.

LISBETH ZWERGER lives in Vienna where she studied at the Academy of Arts before beginning her career as a freelance artist. She has illustrated many highly successful picture books, including fairy tales by the Brothers Grimm and Hans Christian Andersen. With books published in more than twenty countries, she has been honoured with many Austrian and foreign awards, including several prizes at the Bologna Children's Book Fair and at the Biennial of Illustrations Bratislava, and the 1980 Hans Christian Andersen Award.